Liberated Publishing Inc

Presents…

I0181752

Married but Single

www.liberatedpublishing.com

Liberated Publishing Inc.
1860 Wilma Rudolph Blvd
Clarksville, TN 37040

ISBN 978-0-9895732-4-5

First Printing: July 2014

Printed in the United States of America

To God I give all the honor, the praise, and the glory for what He has done. For without Him nothing would be possible.

Dedication

I dedicate this book to my husband, my best half, Carl. God's word says in Proverbs 18:22, "he who finds a wife finds a good thing and obtains favor from the Lord". Carl you are the favored of the Lord. It's a privilege to share my life and love with you. You have been my partner in life since 1997 "for better or worse". Our marriage has been tested time and time again which leads me to believe what the devil meant for evil God means for good. God has and will continue to replace, restore, and multiply 100-fold the years the locust have eaten. God wants our union to stand as a testimony before many of His love and faithfulness. We are His and nothing can separate us from His love or for that matter each other. I stand in awe of your faithfulness, patience, understanding, and unconditional love for me. I am truly blessed! My prayer and hearts cry is that we continue to grow stronger and stronger in eternal love.

Love your wifey

Introduction

Hmm. What a title: *Married but Single*. What exactly does that mean? How can you be single, if you're married? You may be thinking I mean common law marriage. Maybe you think I mean you're married, separated, and living your life as if you're single. Well, none of those apply to what I mean by, *Married but Single*. Let me elaborate. You're actually married to the man of your dreams. You know, your God-given "he who finds a wife finds a good thing" man of your dreams. The one God has been preparing you for all of your life.

You both say, "I do.

And then he doesn't.

He doesn't fulfill your emotional needs. He doesn't nurture the heart that he promised to take care of until death do you part. What he does do is drop it.

Now normally when you drop something what do you do? Right! You pick it up, he doesn't. So therefore he doesn't even know that when he dropped your heart, he cracked it. Now because of the crack in your heart, loneliness has crept in.

Let's define the word loneliness. Loneliness is a complex and usually unpleasant emotional response to isolation or lack of companionship. Loneliness typically includes anxious feelings about a lack of connectedness or communality with other beings. Loneliness can be felt even when surrounded by other people or in this case your mate. Loneliness is prevalent in many marriages. One of the things you always hear a single person say is "I just get tired of being alone". Well, there is nothing more worse than a lonely married person who should have that companionship that most single people long for.

You think once you say, "I do" you're on your way to Happyville. News flash some end up on an unexpected detour route to

7

Lonelyville. You may see a sign that says ,"Detour 500 Ft.' and unknowingly may end up taking the detour route from a happy, fulfilling marriage and traveling the scary, dark route of Lonelyville.

What causes this detour? Could it be that you and your mate stopped communicating? Did sexual intimacy cease? Was there an issue that created a sense of betrayal or distrust? Whatever the situation you and your mate may have become lost together and can't find your way back to each other and that thing that made you love each other in the beginning.

There will be other couples on this route so pass with care. Sadly some stay on this road that ends in love's demise and leads to divorce, split families and much emotional heartbreak. Just know you do not have to stay on this path that can lead to years of unhappiness.

There are signs posted as you travel this painful, solitude and sometimes dark path called Lonleyville . These signs are small gems, and small sources of light that when heeded can lead you back to the road of marital bliss and happiness. Follow these signs and you and your mate can again join hands and continue on a beautiful journey of love.

Part I. Danger: Communication Lacking

One of the signs says, "Lack of Communication." Everyone knows that in any relationship you must have communication. Most women feel they have this area covered. When we communicate with our husbands we tell them the whole story.

When I say the whole story, I mean the whole story. They may ask one question like, 'How was your day?' and God knows we can really make them regret ever asking us that question. We will tell them every detail from the time we woke up, until the precise moment we're talking to them.

Most men are totally different. They give one-word answers but we want them to communicate with us the way we communicate with them. We as women want all the juicy details.

Have you ever tried talking to a wall? I haven't either, but I'm sure it was times you felt like you might as well had just spoken to a wall than your husband. At least then you would know why you weren't getting a response. Maybe you felt like you were your spouse's dentist-- pulling teeth for a conversation. You may constantly ask him, "Are you listening?"

Maybe you do have a spouse that does communicate but just not with you. Have you ever heard your spouse talking on the phone and you're looking at the clock like they have been talking for over thirty-minutes. And who do you hear doing all the talking? Your spouse. It's frustrating, when you can't even get a three-minute conversation out of them.

You express to your mate how that makes you feel. You ask them how can they hold a conversation with someone on the phone and not with you. Then you get the same reply, "I do talk to you." I think they figure because they can hear that their listening and because they say, "un huh" and "un un" that means they are now engaging in a conversation. They feel like they "talk" but they don't realize they fail to "communicate".

9

You let them know how critical communication is and that it is the foundation in your relationship. They may say "I'll do better" but better just gets worse.

Your thirst for conversation never gets quenched and causes dryness in your foundation. Soon you realize your relationship is starting to have multiple cracks. The relationship is fragile. The lack of communication leaves you feeling, *Married but Single*.

You feel you can't communicate with your spouse and that may lead to you talking about your spouse to someone who can't fix the problem or ultimately become a part of the problem, if you know what I mean.

At this moment you're in a vulnerable state. You're not getting what you desire from your mate but you do find it in the opposite sex. The opposite sex knows exactly what you need and how you need it. They hear, listen, talk, and communicate all too well. Now, the bible (ISV) says in Ephesians 4:27, "and do not give the devil an opportunity to work." With that being said, the only two people that can fix your lack of communication are you and your spouse.

When the communication begins to suffer, heed the signs and take swift actions to remove communication barriers.
How? By knowing your mate. When is or isn't the right time to talk. Here are our personal techniques of communication.

Our Personal Techniques

In my opinion, communication is something that you have to become skilled at. My best half and I had to learn (and still learning) to asks ourselves: who, what, when, where, and how to communicate with each other. Key word in that sentence was "with." A lot of times we can talk "at" our spouse.

Who: Who is right and who is wrong? Believe it or not my motto was, "Even when I'm wrong I'm right," or "Do a DNA on it and it will come back 99.9 percent right." Honestly, I would be as wrong as two plus two equals five. I realized that although he handled things differently than I did or have an opposing thought, it did not mean that he was wrong.

What: What needs to be discussed and what doesn't? I had to pick and choose my battles. I had to think before I spoke to him and weigh my words carefully. I asked myself: will my words be encouraging or will they pour more fuel on the fire?

When: When is the perfect time to talk? When is a time that would not be productive to talk to him? Shortly after he comes through the door from work was not the perfect time. He needed that cool off/transition period and by allowing him that time, it protected me from feeling *Married but Single*. Choose your when carefully. For example, If your spouse is upset at the moment and talking right then will only escalate the problem, wait for them to have their cool off moment so that the matter can come to a resolution.

Where: Where is the best place to discuss an issue? The location was always a big issue for me and not so much for my husband. I had a big issue with someone trying to check me in a public setting. I felt we should wait until we were in a private setting before communicating about an issue. If your spouse is a private person then wait until you get home or alone to have a discussion.

How: How I opened up the conversation would automatically cause him to be defensive. For example by "you are" instead of "I feel". For me it was talking loudly. Now you understand what I was saying in the "where". He felt like if he talked loud enough he could get his point across better. In actuality it would cause me to shut down and not want to hear anything else he had to say. Do what works in a conversation so that what is being said can be received.

Those are just some techniques that got us on the road to establishing healthy communication.

11

Some other important keys to us:

Pray together.

Asking for forgiveness immediately

Discuss the matter at hand. Don't bring up past issues into the present conversation because the subject at hand often times didn't get resolved.

Never use the silent treatment.

Agree to resolve the issue before going to bed even if you have to agree to disagree.

Saying fewer words is an important key so that he doesn't lose interest in the conversation. We as women can babble, go on and on. Some men just want the main details, the heart of the matter. Every day we are learning to understand each other better and accept each other viewpoint. We are learning to listen without judging and giving our undivided attention.

Scriptures to meditate on:

Proverbs 15:1 A soft answer turneth away wrath: but grievous words stir up anger.

Ephesians 4:29 Let no corrupt communication proceed out of your mouth, but that which is good to the use of edifying, that it may minister grace unto the hearers.

James 1:19 Wherefore, my beloved brethren, let every man be swift to hear, slow to speak, slow to wrath:

Colossians 4:6 Let your words always be gracious, seasoned with salt, so that you will know how you should answer each person.

Proverbs 15:1 "An answer, when mild, turns away rage, but a word causing pain makes anger to come up."

QUESTIONS

How does lack a of communication make you feel Married but Single?

_____

_____

_____

_____

What would make you a better communicator?

_____

_____

_____

Communication is critical. What techniques can you and your mate establish to make it healthier?

_____

_____

_____

_____

When a disagreement happens how can you apply: who, what, when, where, and how, to quickly and fairly dissolve the issue?

_____

_____

_____

_____

Which scripture would you like to work on apply and what course of action will help you apply it?

_____

_____

_____

_____

Pt. II Stop: Romance fades

You're continuing to travel on the road of Lonelyville, you see a second sign that says, "No Romance".

Romance is what builds the relationship. It keeps the relationship, love and passion alive. It is the fire that keeps the logs burning. I I remember asking my best-half when we first met if he was a romantic guy and his reply was, "Yes, I'm very romantic."

We definitely had two different meanings of romance. Let me define the real meaning.

My favorite definition of romance is: "True romance is doing something special or unexpected for someone you love, even though you don't have to. Romance isn't a greeting card. It isn't Valentine's Day. It isn't a box of chocolates, and it certainly isn't a dozen roses (unless you like that sort of thing).

Real romance is not what modern society has been taught to think it is. Real romance isn't manufactured. It is completely individual. Romance is showing the person you love that you're thinking about them. It shouldn't feel forced. There are no limits to romance; it can be shown by a handwritten note, going for a walk, or even by making someone a sandwich.

Romance is something simple and sweet that reminds your partner why they fell in love with you in the first place.
That definition from surprisingly, "The Urban Dictionary," are my exact thoughts of what being a romantic person is all about. It truly is the little meaningful things that count. I don't believe you need a man-made day set aside in order to show your spouse that you love them or that you are thinking of them.

I do believe that whatever you were doing romantically to get your mate, you should continue to do once you have them. Don't blow the candle out after the honeymoon is over. If the real you is not as romantic as you once were or you have allowed the romance to extinguish that could leave your partner saying, "There's just no fire there," "My mate doesn't love me anymore," or even "It feels like we're roommates."

Have you ever said or felt like that? Have you felt like everything was dry except for your pillowcase at night? What about standing on the outside of your relationship looking in at your partner do all the things for others that he or she doesn't do for you?

For example, you may have felt that your spouse goes out of their way to be thoughtful and put a smile on someone else's face. Meanwhile, there's a frown on yours. Maybe your spouse will spend hours of their time with a friend or relative and it's the same time you've asked for.

Reflecting back on my own relationship, I remember my husband and I making plans to go to the movies one night. That evening he left with a relative and did not make it back home until the movies was over. Now granted, I had already been starving for time. It made matters worse when he forgot about our romantic quality time. I definitely let the grits hit the fan that night! I felt, *Married but Single*. I expressed how he made me feel. I had no problem with him spending time with family and friends or even doing thoughtful things for them. The problem occurred when I felt he was so busy doing for others that he forgot about taking care of home first. That night, I got in my car and drove, cried and talked to God. I was telling God on him.

After about a couple of hours of riding, I stopped at taco bell for a Strawberry Fruitista freeze on my way back home. I paid for it and as the guy is handing me my beverage I notice it's just a few strawberries on top. I'm become upset and get ready to tell him he needs to fix it the way it looks on the picture. Right when I'm about to open my mouth, he hands me another one and says, "I'm not sure who fixed this one, because they did not put enough strawberries on top. So I fixed you another one the right way and you can have both of them." I told him thank you. I heard God say, "When you close your mouth, I'll give you double for your

18

trouble." All I could do is pull off smiling while thanking God! Here I am telling God about my husband and God is telling me about myself. That's just like God. The words He spoke ministered right to my heart. I came home, apologized, cuddled, and got romance time after all.

A lot of times we have this painted storybook picture of what romance should look like or how it should be this Cinderella story. Maybe we're looking at a friend's relationship and how romantic their spouse treats them which leave you aweing over their relationship. Then when we're giving something that doesn't look like the romantic picture we envisioned or see we are left feeling married but single. This feeling causes us to speak death over our marriage instead of speaking life.

That's what God meant by "when I close my mouth." By us always speaking against our mate or saying what they never do can cause them to shut down and not do. We also tie God's hands. Now my best half use to give me flowers all the time and tried to shop (clothes, shoes) for me. I told him buying flowers is a waste of money and shopping for me was definitely a no, no. Did this cause the fire to go out? That was the question I had to ask myself. Another question I had to ask myself was, 'What was I doing to romance him?' I think, we, as women want to be given all the romance without reciprocating it. After all love is a two-way street. So what I began to do was close my mouth and started romancing him the way I wanted to be romanced.
That little spark caused a blaze.

Every marriage needs romance. No one wants to live with their spouse feeling like they're roommates. One way to avoid that is by not setting high expectations from your mate that will only leave you disappointed. Your partner's romance strategy may be very different from your own. We were each created uniquely and when it comes to romancing your spouse what we like may be very different from what our partner likes so therefore you may get a different response. Accept your partner's way of expressing his love toward you. Do not look at another person's relationship desiring to have what they have. That can cause you to have higher expectations from your mate. Create your own "awe" moments. Your spouse may not be a fairytale prince or princess but they are your real life prince and princess that may fall short because they are human. Know that "We come to love not by finding a perfect person, but by learning to see an imperfect person perfectly." -Sam Keen

Here are some of the do's we do to keep our romance burning:

We spend time doing what the other one likes to do. I didn't wait for him to "woo" me. If I wanted romance, then I lit the fire

Throughout the day we text each other little messages which builds up our excitement to see each other and it's also a remainder that we are on each other's mind.

We go for walks and talk while holding hands. We are sharing ourselves by talking about our plans dreams and our future while being affectionate.

We do one thing that's spontaneous for each other.

We have date night. It's our priority that we have alone time and enjoy each other's company.

Appreciation is definitely a log we throw on the fire. We let each other know what we admire about each other and appreciate. One thing I had to let my husband know that I do appreciate his way of showing me that he's thinking of me when he gives me flowers. We make sure we don't place one another on the outside looking in position.

We make sure we are each other's partner. Life can be hard sometimes so we have to encourage and build each other up.

Keep each other covered in prayer.

Most importantly we tell each other we love each other and show it. Do you agree that Jacob was one man that showed a woman just how much he really loved her? Genesis 29:20

Scriptures to meditate on

Proverbs 30:18-19 There are three things that amaze me--no, four things that I don't understand: how an eagle glides through the sky, how a snake slithers on a rock, how a ship navigates the ocean, how a man loves a woman.

Song of Solomon 1:2 Kiss me and kiss me again, for your love is sweeter than wine.

Song of Solomon 2:16 My lover is mine, and I am his.

Song of Solomon 8:6 Place me like a seal over your heart, like a seal on your arm; for love is as strong as death, its jealousy unyielding as the grave. It burns like blazing fire, like a mighty flame.

Song of Solomon 8:7 Many waters cannot quench love, neither can floods drown it. If a man offered for love all the wealth of his house, he would be utterly despised.

Questions

How does a lack of romance make you feel Married but Single?

_____

_____

_____

_____

What is your definition of a romantic relationship?

_____

_____

_____

What steps can you and your spouse take to enhance or reignite romance in your marriage?

_____

_____

_____

_____

Have you asked your spouse how he or she would like to experience romance from you?

_____

_____

_____

_____

What three acts of romance would you like to do for your spouse in the next three months?

_____

_____

_____

_____

Pt. III Risk Ahead: Non-sexual intimacy

You're still traveling on this long Lonelyville detour road. You see a warning sign that says, "Risk Ahead", you continue to drive but with caution. You see another sign that says," Lack of Non-Sexual Intimacy".

A lack of non-sexual intimacy can cause the flasher warning lights to come on and cause the sexual intimacy sign to react. Often the two are tied together. I think women, in particular, want to have emotional intimacy and if there is a disconnect then that may cause her to shut down. I'm not saying that men will not shut down sexually. Maybe he does if he feels unappreciated or if he constantly is put down.

For the most part I think most women yearn for non-sexual affection. I know that I did. I use to feel used when every affectionate touch led to sex. I wanted that non-sexual affection shown to me apart from sex, after all, intimacy is so much more than just sex. When I wasn't receiving that intimacy, when the bedroom door closed I would close myself off from him. The walls began to go up. Withdrawal was setting in and my sex drive was diminishing. Sexual intimacy became obligated sex.
I felt married but single.

I think withdrawal and the silent treatment for most women is an indicator that they have been hurt by their spouse. It can also be a danger signal for our spouses. In order to break through this wall, men must begin to show non-sexual intimacy. For me it was foreplay, on the opposite side of the closed door. I do believe that foreplay is not something you just keep in the bedroom. Foreplay should be shown all day long outside of the bedroom which then leads to sexual intimacy in the bedroom. Your daytime relationship can weigh in on your nighttime relations. Feeling loved can lead to sex. Can you recall a time your spouse showed affection all day long or did something for you that was so sweet it made you think, "Oh it's going down tonight". Maybe you can recall a time it was date night and the two of you were having

27

dinner. The whole day was perfect and you are sitting across from your mate thinking how sexy they are looking and how you can't wait to get them to the boom, boom room.

Sex and love go hand-in-hand. Men have sex to show their love and women need to feel loved in order to have sex. Sexual intimacy does bring closeness in our relationships. Non-sexual intimacy can bring separation. A marriage with love without sex can survive but a marriage with sex without love cannot survive. I think that depends on who you are asking, the husband or the wife.

Sex is vital and it is one thing you cannot withhold from your spouse despite how they are making you feel. The first thing we as women want to do is put a lock on the cookie jar. 1Corinthians 7:5 tells us not to withhold ourselves from one another. Remember Satan is always lurking and ready to cause division especially in marriages, your marriage in particular. He knows that sexual intimacy is a bonding force created by God. If you are withholding sex from your spouse then you should be seeing a sign with bright flashing red lights that says, "Danger".

The route I took to get off this non-sexual intimacy detour

First I started initiating what I wanted by doing it. It helped eliminate the wall that caused isolation in the bedroom. For example, before my epiphany if we were lying in the bed and I wanted to be held, I would wait for him to grab and hold me. When that didn't happen that non-sexual emotion would spark and there went up a wall. I realized I didn't have to wait on him to always fulfill my needs. By me initiating, it cut out a lot of the bedroom drama.

We had to become a student of each other. Neither one of us are mind readers. I couldn't expect him to know what I wanted and how. I recall one time telling my best half all the "don'ts", you don't do this and you don't that. His is reply was, "Well teach me the do's. Teach me how to love you." Him just saying that was a

28

non-sexual touch.

We had to be willing to learn how to please each other. In irony, we are both trying to arrive at the same place (the boom, boom room). Men tend to arrive a little quicker since they are aroused visually. It takes us women a little longer. We're like tea pots, you have to warm us up and then we'll blow.

Have a selfless attitude. We had to understand that everything we needed non-sexually and sexually lie within each other. When one of us desires a need we cannot be selfish and not willing to fulfill that need.

I had to learn to wave my flag before it got bad so that sex wouldn't be used as a weapon.

We had to both be willing to become and be builders. Building oneness in our marriage helped us to become "one flesh."
A little nugget- After a heated discussion, HAVE SEX! Everyone knows that make-up sex is the best sex.

Scriptures to meditate on

1 Corinthians 7:2-3 But because of the temptation to sexual immorality, each man should have his own wife and each woman her own husband. Let the husband render unto the wife due benevolence: and likewise also the wife unto the husband.

Ephesians 5:21 Submitting yourselves one to another in the fear of Christ.

Ephesians 5:25 Husbands, love your wives, just as Christ also loved the church, and gave Himself up for her;

Colossians 3:18 Wives, be subject to your husbands, as is fitting in the Lord.

1 Peter 3:7 Likewise, husbands, live with your wives in an understanding way, showing honor to the woman as the weaker vessel, since they are heirs with you of the grace of life, so that your prayers may not be hindered.

Questions

How has having a lack of non-sexual intimacy made you feel Married but Single?

_____

_____

_____

_____

What bricks don't your spouse use that you use to build up a wall?

_____

_____

_____

What initiation can you make to prevent "the bedroom wall"?

_____

_____

_____

_____

Your spouse is the student, what do you want to teach them about non-sexual intimacy?

_____

_____

_____

_____

What have you learned about yours spouse's non-sexual intimacy needs and how can you fulfill them?

_____

_____

_____

_____

Pt. IV Detour Ending

You and your spouse see a sign that says, "Detour Ending." Now we all know how it feels to see a sign that we want to see after being rerouted. We may say, "Whew! That was a long detour" or "That wasn't that bad." It just all depends on how fast or slow you drove through the route and how long of a route the detour was. But just know, God designed the detour for a purpose. God knows exactly what He is doing within your union. We must be willing to yield and allow Him to lead our direction. The story of the Israelites is one example.

Exodus 13:17-18 When Pharaoh finally let the people go, God did not lead them along the main road that runs through Philistine territory, even though that was the shortest route to the Promised Land. God said, "If the people are faced with a battle, they might change their minds and return to Egypt." But God led the people around by the way of the wilderness toward the Red Sea. And the people of Israel went up out of the land of Egypt equipped for battle.

That was a God designed detour. It was also one of His most powerful miracles. Don't despise the detours in your marriages. Allow God to show Himself powerful.

The detours in our marriage only made us stronger.

I can attest to not just one but many detours. I realized detours are for a purpose. We could be heading toward a disaster unaware of the pending danger and God has to allow a detour route to prevent the plan of the enemy in our marriage. But with each detour God had His hand on us. He didn't allow us to get lost on the route. He had people in place to help guide us into the right direction. The detours were not designed to destroy us although that was the plan of the enemy. The detours made us an even stronger power couple. We had to learn to be passengers and allow God to take the wheel.

35

Scriptures to meditate on

Psalm 37:23-24 The LORD directs the steps of the godly. He delights in every detail of their lives. Though they stumble, they will never fall, for the LORD holds them by the hand.

Proverbs 3:6 In all your ways submit to him, and he will make your paths straight.

Isaiah 59:19 When the enemy shall come in like a flood, the Spirit of the LORD shall lift up a standard against him

Romans 8:28 And we know that God causes everything to work together for the good of those who love God and are called according to his purpose for them.

1 Corinthians 10:13 The temptations in your life are no different from what others experience. And God is faithful. He will not allow the temptation to be more than you can stand. When you are tempted, he will show you a way out so that you can endure.

1 Peter 1:7 These trials will show that your faith is genuine. It is being tested as fire tests and purifies gold--though your faith is far more precious than mere gold. So when your faith remains strong through many trials, it will bring you much praise and glory and honor on the day when Jesus Christ is revealed to the whole world.

Questions

What ways can you allow God to be the driver of your marriage so you?

_____

_____

_____

_____

How has a detour route made your marriage stronger?

_____

_____

_____

What do you want God to do within your marriage?

_____

_____

_____

_____

What detours have you and your spouse faced and how will you handle them if they occur again?

_____

_____

_____

_____

What positive things came from the last detour you've had in your marriage?

_____

_____

_____

_____

Happyville

You finally see a sign that says, "End of Construction" followed by a sign that says, "Now entering Happyville: For better or worse."

Soon after you see "Welcome to Happyville" with their state motto that says, "If you want happiness within your marriage look inward."

Most of us think that marriage will bring us happiness. It won't. Once the initial high wears off you will still be you but with twice as much baggage.

Have you ever told your spouse "You don't make me happy" or "I'm just not happy with you"? I use to tell my best half that all the time. When we were separated living apart from each other I was still not "happy" which I should've been if I'm no longer living with the person that I thought was causing my unhappiness. It occurred to me that it was not him. It was me.

He was doing everything to try to make me happy. No matter what he would've done, it still wouldn't have made me happy.

In Genesis 2:18 God said, "It is not good that the man should be alone; I will make a helper who is just right for him." God did not go on to say, "And the two of them shall make each other happy."

When I was looking outward expecting my husband or things to make me happy I was vulnerable, easily hurt, and feeling married but single.

When happiness didn't come. I realized being married was not the key to my happiness and my husband was not the primary source for making me happy. Happiness is a state of mind, an emotion something that is intangible. So, I had to plug into the real source of my joy (God), look deep within, and find inner peace and healing for my emotional wounds.

Wholeness to happiness

Happiness is something you yourself bring into the marriage. The point of marriage isn't to find our other half so therefore, you cannot expect your partner to make you whole. You both must come into the marriage whole knowing that your happiness as an individual and as a partner comes from within. When you're happy you spread happiness and being happy is just one key ingredient to exist with your partner in Happyville.

Scriptures to meditate on

Nehemiah 8:10 Do not grieve, for the joy of the LORD is your strength."

Psalm 34:18 The LORD is close to the brokenhearted; he rescues those whose spirits are crushed.

Romans 15:13 May the God of hope fill you with all joy and peace in believing, so that by the power of the Holy Spirit you may abound in hope.

2 Corinthians 7:4 Great is my boldness of speech toward you, great is my glorying of you: I am filled with comfort, I am exceeding joyful in all our tribulation.

2 Thessalonians 3:16 Now may the Lord of peace himself give you peace at all times and in every way. The Lord be with all of you

Questions

How has a lack of happiness in your marriage made you feel Married but single?

_____

_____

_____

_____

How did you become whole in order to have happiness or how did being whole make you happy?

_____

_____

_____

_____

What makes you happy?

_____

_____

_____

_____

When you are feeling unhappy, what do you feel has to be done in order for your happiness to return?

_____

_____

_____

_____

What can your spouse do to add to your happiness?

_____

_____

_____

_____

Closing thoughts

A good marriage is only as strong as its foundation. Solid marriages are built on the firm foundation of Christ.
Psalms 127:1 says, "Unless the LORD builds the house, They labor in vain who build it;'

The two must become one and build on that oneness for a lifetime totally relying on God and having a solid commitment of unconditional love. Romance is an outward expression of that love. The fire in the fireplace. Make it a point to have communication, romance, and non-sexual intimacy a part of your everyday diet by talking more, kissing more, hugging more, and touching. Let your spouse know that "yes we may have struggles, but I love you." Know that we are responsible for our own happiness. Emotional wounds can become toxic wounds and will have you carrying your broken heart in your hands expecting your mate to repair what you thought they cracked when in reality it was already broken before the marriage.

Beware of road signs in your marriage

While you are traveling down the marriage road beware of the signs along the way. The signs will give you direction from your spouse. Write what each sign would mean in your marriage

Song of Solomon poems

The Bridegroom Praises the Bride

Behold, thou art fair, my love;
behold, thou art fair;
thou hast doves' eyes within thy locks:
thy hair is as a flock of goats,
that appear from mount Gil'e-ad.

Thy teeth are like a flock of sheep that are even shorn,
which came up from the washing;
whereof every one bear twins,
and none is barren among them.

Thy lips are like a thread of scarlet,
and thy speech is comely:
thy temples are like a piece of a pomegranate within thy locks.

Thy neck is like the tower of David builded for an armory,
whereon there hang a thousand bucklers,
all shields of mighty men.

Thy two breasts are like two young roes that are twins,
which feed among the lilies.

Until the day break,
and the shadows flee away,
I will get me to the mountain of myrrh,
and to the hill of frankincense.
Thou art all fair, my love;
there is no spot in thee.

Come with me from Lebanon, my spouse,
with me from Lebanon:
look from the top of Ama'na,
from the top of Shenir and Hermon,
from the lions' dens,
from the mountains of the leopards.

Thou hast ravished my heart, my sister, my spouse;
thou hast ravished my heart with one of thine eyes,
with one chain of thy neck.
How fair is thy love, my sister, my spouse!
How much better is thy love than wine!
and the smell of thine ointments than all spices!

Thy lips, O my spouse, drop as the honeycomb:
honey and milk are under thy tongue;
and the smell of thy garments is like the smell of Lebanon.
A garden inclosed is my sister, my spouse;
a spring shut up, a fountain sealed.

Thy plants are an orchard of pomegranates, with pleasant fruits;
camphire, with spikenard,
spikenard and saffron;
calamus and cinnamon,
with all trees of frankincense;
myrrh and aloes,
with all the chief spices:
a fountain of gardens,
a well of living waters,
and streams from Lebanon.

Awake, O north wind;
and come, thou south;
blow upon my garden,
that the spices thereof may flow out.
Let my beloved come into his garden,
and eat his pleasant fruits.

I am come into my garden, my sister, my spouse:
I have gathered my myrrh with my spice;
I have eaten my honeycomb with my honey;
I have drunk my wine with my milk.
Eat, O friends; drink,
yea, drink abundantly, O beloved.

The Bride Praises the Bridegroom

What is thy beloved more than another beloved,
O thou fairest among women?
What is thy beloved more than another beloved,
that thou dost so charge us?

My beloved is white and ruddy,
the chiefest among ten thousand.
His head is as the most fine gold;
his locks are bushy, and black as a raven:
his eyes are as the eyes of doves by the rivers of waters,
washed with milk, and fitly set:
his cheeks are as a bed of spices, as sweet flowers:
his lips like lilies, dropping sweet smelling myrrh:
his hands are as gold rings set with the beryl:
his belly is as bright ivory overlaid with sapphires:
his legs are as pillars of marble, set upon sockets of fine gold:
his countenance is as Lebanon, excellent as the cedars:
his mouth is most sweet:
yea, he is altogether lovely.
This is my beloved, and this is my friend,
O daughters of Jerusalem.

Love Quotes

A husband can love his wife best when he loves God first –
Unknown

A wise woman builds her home –Proverbs 14:1

And now these three remain: Faith, hope, and love. But the
greatest of these is love. –Holy Bible

A successful marriage requires falling in love many times, always
with the same person
–Mignon McLaughlin

Real love? It's when you go through the hard trial of trust and
sacrifice and still wake up every morning falling in love all over
again –Unknown

A happy marriage is the union of two good forgivers –Ruth Bell
Graham

How do you spell love? –Piglet
You don't spell it…you feel it. –Pooh

 The one thing we can never get enough of is love. And the one
thing we never give enough is love.
–Henry Miller

Love me when I least deserve it because that's when I really need
it –Swedish Proverb

Remember, we're madly in love, so it's alright to kiss me anytime
you feel like it –Peeta, Hunger Games

Real love is when you go through the toughest storm and find
yourself still holding hands when you come out -Unknown

Sometimes our toughest challenges turn out to be our greatest blessings. –Billy Cox

If it doesn't break your heart, it isn't love. -Jon Foreman

Everyone wants happiness, no one wants pain. But you can't make a rainbow, without a little rain
-Unknown

Every test in our life makes us bitter or better, every problem comes to break us or make us. The choice is ours whether we become VICTIM or VICTOR –Alexander Alvarez

Through weakness and strength, happiness and sorrow, for better or worse, I will love you with every beat of my heart -Unknown

Where there is great love there is always miracles –Willa Cather

Marriage is a mosaic you build with your spouse. Millions of tiny moments that create your love story
–Jennifer Smith

WHAT EVERY KISS MEANS:

- Kiss on the Stomach... I'm ready
- Kiss on the Forehead... I hope we're together forever
- Kiss on the Ear... You are my everything
- Kiss on the Cheek... You look so cute
- Kiss on the Hand... I adore you
- Kiss on the Neck... We belong together
- Kiss on the Shoulder... I want you
- Kiss on the Lips... I love you

WHAT THE GESTURE MEANS:

- Holding Hands... We definitively like each other
- Soft slap on the Butt... That's mine
- Holding on Tight... I don't want you to let go
- Looking into each other's Eyes... I just plainly love you
- Playing with Hair... Tell me you love me
- Arms around the Waist... I love you too much to let go
- Laughing while Kissing... I am totally comfortable with you

TWO ADVICES:
1. Don't ask for a kiss, take one!
2. If you were thinking about someone while reading this, you are definitively in love!

ALL THIS APPLIES TO MEN AND WOMEN

Women's keywords and their meaning.

"Fine": This is the word women use at the end of any argument when they feel they are right but need to shut the man up. Men will never be allowed to end a sentence with the word "fine" and just walk away, this word is for the sole use of women in this context. Oh, and by the way, (refer to the definition of "Oh" below), NEVER use "fine" to describe how a woman looks, or in about "five minutes" (see below also), you will hear the word "Fine" followed by silence.

"Five minutes": This is half an hour. It is equivalent to the five minutes that your football game is going to last before you take out the trash, so she feels that it's an even trade.

"Nothing": This means something and you should be on your toes. "Nothing" is usually used to describe the feeling a woman has of wanting to turn you inside out, upside down, and backwards. "Nothing" usually signifies an argument that will last "Five Minutes" and end with the word "Fine".

"Go Ahead" (with raised eyebrows): This is a dare. One that will result in a woman getting upset over "Nothing" and will end with the word "Fine".

"Go Ahead" (with normal eyebrows): This means "I give up" or "do what you want because I don't care". You will get a Raised Eyebrow "Go Ahead" in just a few minutes, followed by "Nothing" and "Fine" and she will talk to you in about "Five Minutes" when she cools off.

A Loud Sigh: This is not actually a word, but is still often a verbal statement very misunderstood by men. A "Loud Sigh" means she thinks you are an idiot at that moment and wonders why she is wasting her time standing here and arguing with you over "Nothing".

A Soft Sigh: Again, not a word, but a verbal statement. "Soft Sighs" are one of the few things that some men actually understand. She is content. Your best bet is to not move or breathe and she will stay content.

"Oh": This word followed by any statement is trouble. Example; "Oh, I talked to John about what you two were doing last night". If she says "Oh, by the way" before a statement, run, do not walk, to the nearest exit. When she is done tossing your clothes out the window, she will tell you that she is "Fine" but do not expect her to talk to you for at least 2 days. "Oh" as a question, as in, "Oh??!!" usually signifies that you are caught in a lie. Do not try to lie more to get out of it, or you will get a Raised Eyebrows "Go ahead" followed by acts so unspeakable that I can't bring myself to write about them.

"That's Okay": This is one of the most dangerous statements that a woman can say to a man. "That's Okay" means that she wants to think long and hard before paying you retribution for what ever it is that you have done. "That's Okay" is often combined with the word "Fine" and accompanied by the Raised Eyebrow "Go Ahead". At some point, probably without warning, in either the near or distant future (time holds no significance here), you are going to definitely remember this initial moment and regret it. More than likely you will regret it more than once over the duration of your relationship.

"Please Do": This is not a statement, it is an offer. A woman is giving you the chance to come up with whatever excuse or reason you have for doing whatever it is that you have done. You have a fair chance to tell the truth, so be careful and you shouldn't get a "That's Okay" scenario.

"Thanks": A woman is thanking you. Do not faint, just say you're welcome.

"Thanks A Lot": This is much different than "Thanks". A woman will say, "Thanks A Lot" when she is really ticked off at you. It signifies that you have hurt her in some callous way, and will be followed by the

"Loud Sigh". Be careful not to ask what is wrong after the "Loud Sigh", as she will only tell you "Nothing"....see paragraph one.

What men say and what they mean ...

"I'M GOING FISHING" Means: "I'm going to drink myself dangerously stupid, and stand by a stream with a stick in my hand, while the fish swim by in complete safety."

"IT'S A GUY THING" Means: "There is no rational thought pattern connected with it, and you have no chance at all of making it logical."

"CAN I HELP WITH DINNER?" Means: "Why isn't it already on the table?" "UH HUH," "SURE, HONEY," OR

"YES, DEAR..." Means: Absolutely nothing. It's a conditioned response.

"IT WOULD TAKE TOO LONG TO EXPLAIN" Means: "I have no idea how it works."

"I WAS LISTENING TO YOU. IT'S JUST THAT I HAVE THINGS ON MY MIND." Means: "I was wondering if that redhead over there is wearing a bra."

"TAKE A BREAK HONEY, YOU'RE WORKING TOO HARD". Means: "I can't hear the game over the vacuum cleaner." "THAT'S INTERESTING, DEAR." Means: "Are you still talking?"

"YOU KNOW HOW BAD MY MEMORY IS." Means: "I remember the theme song to 'F Troop', the address of the first girl I ever kissed, and the vehicle identification numbers of every car I've ever owned, but I forgot your birthday."

"I WAS JUST THINKING ABOUT YOU, AND GOT YOU THESE ROSES". Means: "The girl selling them on the corner was a real babe."

"OH, DON'T FUSS, I JUST CUT MYSELF, IT'S NO BIG DEAL." Means: "I have actually severed a limb, but will bleed to death before I admit that I'm hurt."

"HEY, I'VE GOT MY REASONS FOR WHAT I'M DOING." Means: "And I sure hope I think of some pretty soon."

"I CAN'T FIND IT." Means: "It didn't fall into my outstretched hands, so I'm completely clueless."

"WHAT DID I DO THIS TIME?" Means: "What did you catch me at?"

"I HEARD YOU." Means: "I haven't the foggiest clue what you just said, and am hoping desperately that I can fake it well enough so that you don't spend the next 3 days yelling at me."

"YOU KNOW I COULD NEVER LOVE ANYONE ELSE." Means: "I am used to the way you yell at me, and realize it could be worse."

"YOU LOOK TERRIFIC." Means: "Please don't try on one more outfit, I'm starving."

"I'M NOT LOST. I KNOW EXACTLY WHERE WE ARE." Means: "No one will ever see us alive again."

"WE SHARE THE HOUSEWORK." Means: "I make the messes, she cleans them up."

Special Thanks

A big thank you goes to Tavia D. Green. Your editing was efficient and professional. Also, a big thank you to Gravityx9. Your graphic design was perfect for my title. You both helped me make my dream come true. You came through for me. Thank you both so very much!

About the author

Michelle E. Medley lives in Tennessee with her husband, four children, and grandson. She is a freelance, writer, and poet. She is the author of, "Inspired from the Secret Place". By no surprise, one of her favorite hobbies is writing. Through her writing, she fulfills her passion to encourage, uplift, and inspire others. Because of her own life experiences she knows that if God can bring her through He will do the same for you. It is just a matter of time. Michelle can be contacted at michelleemedley@yahoo.com

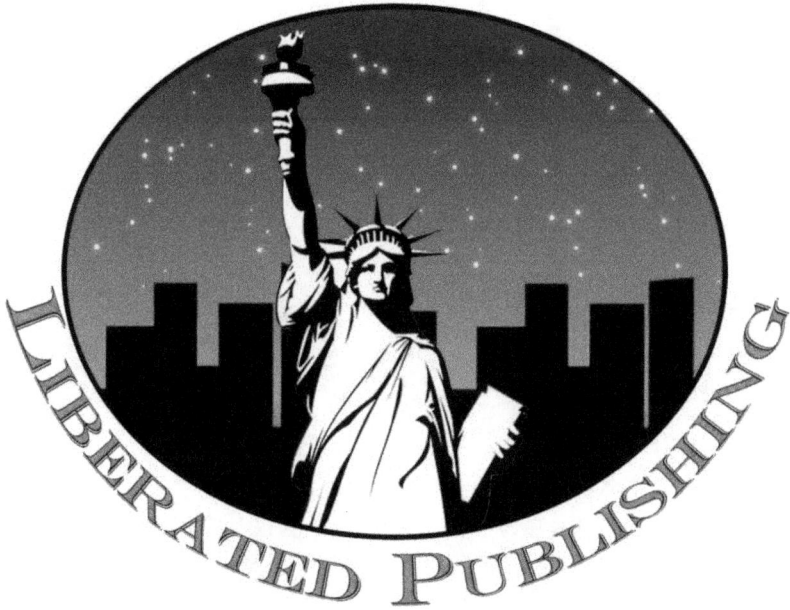

Liberated Publishing Inc
1860 Wilma Rudolph Blvd
Clarksville, TN 37040
info@liberatedpublishing.com
931-378-0500

www.LiberatedPublishing.com